Arabian Nights

Also by Jack Marshall

Arabian Nights

POEMS BY JACK MARSHALL

COFFEE HOUSE PRESS : : MINNEAPOLIS : : 1986

Acknowledgments: Some of these poems have appeared in the following magazines: *American Poetry Review, Pequod, Pivot, Canard Anthology, Confrontation, Zyzzyva.* Of the poems from *The Darkest Continent,* which was published in a limited edition of three hundred copies in 1967 by For Now Press, "The Gold Coast" originally appeared in *New World Writing* #16, and "Crosswinds" and "Park West" appeared in *The Hudson Review.* I would like to thank Donald Phelps, for his invaluable aid in bringing out my first collection, and Robert Vas Dias, for his help in designing it.

The publishers thank the National Endowment for the Arts, a federal agency, for a Small Press Assistance Grant that aided in the production of this book.

Coffee House Press books are available to bookstores and libraries through our primary distributor: Consortium Book Sales & Distribution, 213 East Fourth Street, St. Paul, Minnesota 55101. Our books are also available through most other small-press distributors and through all major library jobbers. For personal orders, catalogs, or other information, write to Coffee House Press, Box 10870, Minneapolis, Minnesota 55440.

Library of Congress Cataloging-in-Publication Data

Marshall, Jack, 1936-
  Arabian nights.

  I. Title.
PS3563.A722A73   1986   811'.54   86-19273
ISBN 0-918273-28-5 (pbk.)

CONTENTS

Arabian Nights

For Naomi
and in memory of my mother,
Grace Marshall
(1905-1986)

Arabian Nights

These two not breathing now once lived
in a house that has no number anymore,

no window looking out on an avenue
only a window can look steadily on…and then,

with clarity, on mostly confusion. No more
third-floor walk-up bricked-in now

above the Mobil gas station, below a neon Pegasus
riding thousands of nights into an afterlife for old autos.

In this photo they smile so easefully
from so far, the past seems

not to have happened yet. So long
ago, before I was born — I can hardly believe

how beautiful they are! Clear
looks in their eyes I keep

looking into and through, I follow
my mother's across in steerage so close to hullside,

she said, you could hear a shark, scavenging for garbage,
being ground up in the propellor;

my father's I follow through sweeping dust
out of piled Persian rugs carpeting the enchanted

lace-curtained clip joints of Fifth Avenue.
His faded immigration photo

showed a swarthy young Arab with a wary look.
This studio pose I've found

shows them in a regal calm I never saw, lost
how or when I hardly have a clue. I wonder,

have their still proud, unruffled foreheads,
his wavy pompadour, her petal-lipped mouth, been retouched?

From his right hand tucked suavely in hip pocket
a black silk stripe unrolls

down his rented tux, a yard of
good luck he'll use up

just in staying alive. In her arms she holds
a dozen large calla lilies in full bloom.

Thirty-Seven

Waking to find yourself the same
age your father was eight years before you
were born,
            and already the massed weight of
your experience shakes you.
Tenderness gone, and longing,
                        though you send it, unspent,
away, won't go.

Your son is somewhere else, so often
is he in your thoughts, and you doubt
he can know this.
Each time you see him feels like the first
                        and last.

Alone in your room,
what do you want of him
alone in his room? — absence
real as any event...
            How being far
from that missed encounter diminishes, fills
you with a lack of,
the courage to care...

                  His is a childhood
not yours, not nearly,
though you would wish it,
and if you were there,
            would again be different.

Now, as when a boy, you fear   5
coming to nothing,
and under the eaves the owl hoots
from the night world still in sight
                        to a sun you woo, unrisen
unless you go down.

LETTER TO MY FATHER ON THE OTHER SIDE

Your nights draw nearer
as your face drifts away.
Though now the Atlantic Ocean stands
between us like frosted glass,
you were never closer...
not even when you approached
to offer me your failing business.

Success! You tried
but lacked the know-how.
Like a kept woman,
thankless, mean, insatiable,
it ate away your life
and what it left was not enough
to meet the sumptuous needs
extorted by the age.

It wasn't long before the squeeze
showed in your shuffling gait;
yet you stayed.
Watching you thin so,
I couldn't help quarreling
and soon left.
Yesterday, passing a dry-goods window
on the Rue St. Jacques,
with stockings much too long
for its plaster foot display
(toeless, just like yours),
brought it back to me:
the dim shop
on the ghost town's edge,
its cramped window dizzy
with Arabic-tipped lettering —

signs you stayed up nights
penning like a scribe –
and you, less lord than janitor,
absently dusting the stacks
of never-diminishing towels,
waiting for the rush.
Instead, stray bargain hunters
came now and then, blinking
like rats;
having no one else, you stayed.

Holding out is everything.
Early today I went back
to see what more I could recognize.
Standing there before the window,
I saw a face, peeled and shopworn
from being too long under the hot lamps,
peer back at me.
Seeing it made me want to write you
after these many years.
Have you taken a room in town yet,
or do you still lay a blanket out
beneath the counter every night?

DEAL

These vast lawns landscaped for show
and seclusion along this prime stretch
of South Jersey Shore, at night elegantly
lit by tall, tapering swan-necked streetlamps;
these grand gingerbread houses are rumored
paid for with coin bags full of slot-machine quarters — skimmed
cream from new casinos, Atlantic
City just down the boardwalk.
Glass-walled, bubble-roofed, up go
honeywood homes built big as luxury
liners. From their windows, owners can see
their ships carrying their cargoes in heavily
insured, cubed containers inching the horizon.
On this blue-chip shore front
colonized by new-rich, first-generation Syrians
whose parents were forties welfare-recipient
immigrants in Eastern and Bay Parkways, Brooklyn,
my widowed mother — uprooted from living more than fifty years
across the street from her once-handsome, proud brother
now a paranoid hermit —
my mother, now more than ever through cataract-clouded
eyes unimpressed by the view, sneers, "Big
deal!"

   Prolonging my yearly visit from summer's magical day-
light savings into suspiring fall's magically reversed standard
time, I need to make the quick miracle
drug, which money is,
and have taken a job working for a scowling
boss who wears an embroidered yarmulke on his head
to mark his humble place beneath the heel of the most high
Allah Elohim. Like Him owner of a time corporation,
he sells shiny jeweled pieces of sun

that tarnish by the gross on wrist and throat and drives
his Russian- and Spanish-speaking women clock punchers
numb.
      Fingers, having to set, stiffen
around a moment, the very heart of time, stalled, then drive
themselves faster in the cold, bleak,
thirty-thousand square-feet shed — stone floor, steel roof — just to keep
from freezing; and even if there were any
heat, it would only rise to the rafters anyway.
Among dials gone dead and quietly wild-
cat pulsing batteries', modules', quartz crystals'
brief lifetimes running down all
around us, he tells me he believes in a life
after death, that his piety ensures
a place there for him. God is his good-
luck charm, long-term banker, and hustling
export agent in Hong Kong, guarantor of never-ending
credit. It is for more of this
each night on the chartered bus home he prays,
then with his pals plays poker with renewed brio.

In my mother's small three-room apartment,
her illegal immigrant Haitian nursemaid,
Carmella, having read her Bible and fanatically
squealed for the blood of a blond
masked wrestler on the all-day TV, chirps her Creole pidgin
and asks me how she can record a message on the same tape
her mother and three children have sent from Port-au-Prince.
She has not seen them in over a year.
Lying on her stomach on the bedroom floor, she plays
the tape over and over, legs lolling side
to side, back and forth, listening
to them in turn speak, in unison sing to her as she
sings along. Behind a shaky, arthritic hand, my mother
jeers, *"Mittle shwayt keleb"* — Arabic

9

for "Like a bunch of dogs" — she calls
children calling their mother, a mother calling her child-
like daughter herself a mother. I too must call
up hand-signed pidginese to answer,
"No record *pas que* tape erase," to which she nods
that helpless, uncomprehending smile,
as when my mother in her own broken
but not inaccurate English tells her
the brand name of the sugar substitute
she wants from the grocer, Sweet 'n' Rough.
After the high-pitched, tropical-plumed
chant of her children's voices, I hear
Carmella's mother repeat a gruff, cautionary
"Mal...mal..." and wonder
what about, and watch her eyes
widen, brow wrinkle, with rapt attention.

Living this past year with my mother, she's given her
each morning the prescribed
injection of twenty units of insulin for her diabetes
and does again: slow swab, quick shot in the thigh,
Mom curses, Carmella gives her laugh,
as when she holds out one
each of the five kinds of pills — each
a different color — with a glass of water
Mom must take before bed; and though she's full
of excuses as I was as a boy,
there's Carmella, nursemaid monitor
of the medicine cup, both hands held out.
Later from my room I hear
Mom scold and tease, and Carmella's mischievous
laugh, and it somehow pleases
and saddens me at once to imagine
this going on before I arrived, wondering
how long it will continue after I leave.

Dawn Notes

By the waters of Deal
we raise our heads,
old saber-
toothed Islamic
moon still
up,
    sun
        not yet

———————

Get up. Go. On the way
don't ask why fatigue hangs
in like a drug
against meaning. Weariness
too may have its uses.
After it, what lasts
is truly yours

———————

Continually as each moment
catches at the edge, space,
your sleep-numbed
fingers are
swimming through

———————

August heat, sluggish heart
grateful for desire
taking the brain
by storm

———————

As seasons are a music,
they wear us down; long
before they begin giving out, we're done
giving in

———————

Though privileged
to be
in on one
more moment
again beginning
beautiful as now
walking
tree-tunneled streets,
leaf-edged sky,
and out from dark fields come
into time

———————

Back on shore
left twenty years ago,
greet that older one
with the younger
returned, redolent
of women ripened
like oranges in Tunisia

———————

Tropic air
hardly stirring
brought over, some flutter
of a breeze now shaking
pennants, scalloped awnings
blue-edged on cabanas
of Deal Casino

———————

Have you ever been anywhere
but within
Arabian
Night

———————

Night, open book,
making equals of all,
nothing hidden, nothing ruled
out for long. What keeps the ocean
back? sky up? earth
from crumbling? Of whom
is there to beg,
be grateful
for all coming on

———————

Night, old
as a mother
who has outlived
all her sons' wives

———————

Pass the red farmhouse,
young divorcee's
upstairs bedroom
window light again
not on

———————

Black silk skullcaps,
strewn shells
on the long quiet
lawns of Deal recall

the nightly overturned
black beetles on the mountain
streets of Jalapa, the sweepers'
twig brooms swept into mounds

———————

What leaves in the light
show red and gold
are in the dark
black
and blue

———————

Each work-
day of the weak
feels like hauling
a whole unfucking week

———————

Caw caw caw — high
in the trees, hooting
birds mimic
a train horn's far
bending
echo

———————

Parked, waiting
behind the wheel
by the railroad side,
a woman, getting ready to board,
brushes on blush
dawn enroses

———————

From Long Branch, Red Bank, Little Silver
mist
through russet leaves, first
taste of rough wine-
tongued October

———————

6:43 a.m. sun-
light flashes
off reflectors on rows
of Jeeps, Fort Monmouth's vast open
motor pool

———————

The two Chicano
field hands in frayed denim
and rope-soled shoes each morning
squatting in front of Sacco's
Landscaping, waiting for the pickup truck —
this morning, where are they?

———————

Elkwood Stables open-
air water trough still,
piled hay, flat turf
in the distance all steam
for the undisturbed
sleepers in their stalls

———————

Eyes closed, softly
sense how, beside you,
eyes open,
sits no one

———————

On stairs, escalator, platform,
women in white
scuffed sneakers, eager for the run
up the executive ladder

———————

In lovely faces, sadness
multiplied
the more it knows
what ruin will bring

———————

Dawn, momentarily
flushing commuter faces
asleep or reading news, rides
us all into the smoky
furnace having no favorites

———————

Day
comes sharpening
its tooth on you and all
happening under clear skies

Leaving Eden

LEAVING EDEN

Reaching the summit, they looked out.
Desert and the far hazy blue
mountains south that had been home.
Below, the winding way they traced
had long ago twisted spiny
briers dry. Wide, blinding light
in place of water. Trees — prehistoric
coiled tails lashed upright — fixed
charred black lightning
on weightless white. To see
and not go back. And how could he
imagine the fate of even the most wary,
wavering hero drawn cunningly out
of hiding, only to be gunned down
in some alley of history, how imagine
that not making the prolonged sweet
time of their lives seem temporary
amnesty? Back in that rain forest
of a garden she would not let him weed
felt like time itself growing. Tiny
bronze bells on her feet when she walked
warned the ants; small running
creatures, shying away, she calmed
and made a place for. He watched, marveling
how one unbroken pulse could be shared
among so many. There were days under the luxuriant
hammer of the sun he felt a tenderness, nearly crippling, expand
and touch what, alone, he would not have dreamed of
approaching. How she nourished each without stinting
any. "Love," he heard there
from whatever had a voice to croak or murmur,   19
"only if you give up your power to draw, will we
have no power to follow."
                    Years later he would remember

a man behind them stumble onto the summit, his face
pulled askew as he swung it, nervously glancing, up, saw her
and was struck. As though, of all things he'd thought
he had outdistanced, she
had beat him there, woman's beauty
hounding still, nearly too much to bear, thousands of feet
in the air, in the flesh, unequal portions
again, pain, paradise, the heart
loses, recovers, loses, re...

Harbor Music

Near the old fishing boats dipping
in oily swells by the worn, wooden pier,
no need eavesdropping to hear

what those blue-haired ladies are saying, dipping
rhythmically and bobbing like oars among shrimp
cocktails cupped in their faltering feminine hands…

Though the air has no petals now
and only the leaf tips on the trees show
amber – "As far as autumn

gets around here" – like petals on the air
the sea breeze brings to ear,
"What do you like in bed,

tea or coffee?" Still such choices left
drifting above running music and the heft-
y tug's wake growing still

powerful
with ever more power to
still the many voices noise uses

to mask the seasons'
wearing down and our own
giving in before the music

runs out – motors, street hawkers, the Human
Jukebox – while around the ankles of a thin Asian
laying out a feast for them, a crowd of stray

mewing pier cats,
their sinewy muscles under sleek flowing
black-brown coats sprung from tunnels and sunken

embankments, have flown
toward roast chicken, a banquet of oriental cuisine
spread on the battered hood of his pickup truck. From where —

unsmiling to smiling passersby — has he come? himself
thinning and near
to being canceled, gaunt chef-to-go

on a house call to his waterfront flock before stepping back
or forth into shadows that take
all in like foliage

to be let go. Is this
Frisco or Lagos? And who
is he? No Buddha

but lean as that other: ageless Gold Coast
guide in a creased fedora, Big John, whose heat-maddened
kitties we were then, more than

twenty years ago, drunken deck hands he led
past moonlit natives wrapped in shrouds,
asleep, or dead mouths open,

gurgling in a ditch. To highlife
he led us, to shantytown,
the dank, earthen beds of scarred-cheeked women,

where love, the darkest
continent, taking us in, nearly blacked us
out. The voyage

22   had come to that.
Now with you under the shadow
of this retaining wall, is it the wraith-like spirit

again of harbors come to let us go? This time,
perhaps, into sunshine purple-rayed
as the aster you pick in the grass and say, "See

how more vividly than there,
among the many from which it came, here
we notice it against this green…This

is the secret of poetry, the mystery
of the real and our being
here, which is not nothing." And though less than

midway to one's end, each movement comes
to be carefully measured
by the effort needed; we are

not ready for it: if we were, it wouldn't be
now; it would be
over…And we move on

to all there is
of all there will be: the silk-corded
sunlight stretching from its source,

brilliance undiminished
against faded harbor sheds,
the dun-colored length of the bullet-

nosed, fish-gilled sub's hull on view
at two dollars a head by the foot of the pier
from where, turning back, it seems all harbors

look alike, alien even to such eyes
native for now as ours,
my Kittay, your Mary-Ann.

THE MONTHS OF LOVE

Lying opposite the sun-
capped church dome gleaming
polished mercury across from

sloping Dolores, amid drifting summer
smells — mown grass, split melon, half
sweet baby's breath, half

briny ocean —

you ask their name,
and she calls the bunched white flowering
sprays on the hedgerow above where you lie

"bridal wreath" as you breathe them in,
and the years laid aside in the long
effort at naming rest easy...

as though the words open
in the air an invisible window that gives
shape and savor to the light coming through,

letting in the half-acrid, half-alluring
scent fluttering promise you used to head for
in the dry or wet street rainbowed

with gasoline you'd get a stinging whiff of,
the streaked gold- and blue-
scaled benzine snake rippling

24   beneath car exhaust, then stop and stare
in aching prepubescent wonder, beguiled by
an airborne, promiscuous desire beginning

to call you out of anonymity's
sterile safety, while blurred
heat lulled asleep all sense but

marvel
            wakening
                        Now as then

sour rot so curiously
mixed with sweet spun
in a breeze from so far back you knew it surely

would outstrip you…

And that which has had so much time
in which to be blown away without
a trace is now

more

than ever
here…And there
on the outskirts,

in the Panhandle jungle, off the Great Highway beach —
windblown, isolate, snagged hidden
behind bushes, sprouting amid the stench

and mechanical gurgling sea roar
of the cypress-screened sewage plant —
where the hovering homosexuals

glide shyly out, smiling   25
their tentative, twisted smiles;
let them seduce one another

behind rocks, tall weeds, on the oil-slick sand,
only let them not be left
untouched, faces in a mist held

skewed in the hands of a force demanding
assent, or else leaving
each to stand alone drawing down

despair like a volley ricocheting
from a sniper's gun...
and in spite of the odds against them,

nowhere too foul – even here!

O stink-awakened season lately begun,
how many can such as we
name of all the things that can stop

us cold? calling
down like a blow to the eyes too late
what we failed to realize –

breasts to see, to hold in the hand, froth
held between lip and tooth, thighs
to caress, and how much courage it must take

those frightened men to step forth,
this woman who does not believe
she is beautiful, to offer

her loveliness in a sheer cotton dress...
And what good if not to free

desire mounting the bone-

dry ladder of the rib cage,
giving, getting, humming-
bird-tongued

head between parted
thighs tasting O good

God!

eye, tongue, nipple
alive
to what
        ever eludes closure

Make, Not Have

It's weird, that time — or gap in time —
midwinter seclusion, unending or starting
over, yourself nearly over-
dosed on cutting loose ego,
when more than ever in confusion comes hastening
doubt that from the start what you took up doing
was needed done, matters, that what you inherit
being alive needs realized desire to keep on
being alive and move you
                            on your way...

                            Now amnesia, aphasia, the break-
down of brain cells all hoot
as you can no more hold
in sequence your last thought, next
move, how long since
in-breath, long drawn, long held,
let go, or bare skin felt mild
warm air bringing the far spring-
cleanings of childhood near, bringing you,
without a step, there...
                        What good
then that gruel from gurus: "To find,
first lose"? Soon enough all you've said
you'll have to vacate and tomorrow give
the lie to what was said today. Lucky if it leaves
anything for the sun to awaken...
                            A step
nearly taken
into speeding mad midday
traffic — the curb dizzying
cliff edge — nearly brings instinct closer
to being less trusted. Attention, scattered, plays

havoc with memory losing
ground to history's
debris, recycled, concrete.
And you wonder if there's still a gift
to be grown
on the grafted limb we make, not have, still
some winding sinewy map-
making nostalgia about
childhood you'd thought you'd mustered
and cashed in, left
to make over, make
more of less,
the curses worse, the laughter better...
                                        How
else the fuck in hell hope to break free of
such disarray and disgust
at how unjust chance is that was once
your ace in the hole, if barely, that now comes
at you blade first, now quickens
you among images fluid as air
as you pass the broken parking lot – wild
thick milky licorice star-
anise tasting of ancestors flowing
time's perfume past you, like your father in the dream
as a young man standing under the awning
of a deserted café, staring
into a Sahara spread to the horizon.

How relieved then you are
called back, how eagerly
look forward to seeing dear ones again, eager
to take on the sore
laboring
blossom so anxious
at the core
of their egos, their stunned, hard-

breathing faces looking for
direction all around, like you, surrounded by
diamonds, least
white of a wave
     top charged by the blue
weight under
red and gold
   leaves glimpsed
      salt of the sea
on Mariposa Street.

    Then may you begin
and, when speaking again, hear
yourself as if spoken to
by a voice from within you but not yourself,
speak of things which, until you hear in human company
and the vast oceanic calm
space that surrounds, you cannot know how far
the world's unfurling, pull of the
spiral cord made colorless through
coiling
and uncoiling, looping
you in even as you waver and fall,
as your heart falls
level with its source
over which the laws of language hardly hold,
sway,
giving way
to the wildness of time, no
help, no hope, no solace, only the moment's
measure found, fit,
before letting go
30 tongue's hold
   on no
    home at all

Contra Don Juan

Could you imagine it were lovelier,
more than having seen her once perfectly
beautiful, to stay and see her imperfectly
grow each day more beautiful?
to let her, through your eyes and her own
strangeness to herself, glimpse
the loveliness you sensed tightly curled in her
unfurl from anxious eyes, knitted brow, and ease
the fear that love leaves
quickest those in greatest need?

And though later on there will come a glow — a vast
cold vacant blue aura bending over
you chosen for jealousy and betrayal — and you'll feel
or somehow know it is yours
to be a servant of reversal,
turned so, then, could you stand
and, no longer in the way, dispossessed,
see how transposing *you* to *I*
would make the self-aggrand-
izing accuser confess?...

Then would you choose not to look
away or not take her back,
not admire nor be enthralled by the arduous clarity
she yields to as to a law made visible, dew-like
sorrow, lens through which she sees
and cannot refuse what craves and frees
her from the constantly massing,
threatening cloud, longing?...

Then would you wish not to know
how, for you too, her glistening cry reaches
in words, for words, toward unbinding ties

for something larger than person, reaches
in order to widen, loosen, before letting go
of what also binds you? Is faithfulness, then, any
more than disdain of what stands naked before you?

May you then know a new way
to regard her who looks elsewhere
than to longing, which is not desire
but being full of distances endlessly adrift
or falling short of the living heat that strikes
close, that we try cutting free of in swift
lust or slow-fading loss while the body aches
and echoes after having been struck…

However long through drought you must wait
until the garden nearly ruined by rain inches closer
to being greener for it,

                wait a little longer…

Walk the same streets as those untouched
by the tenderness of being held, who crouch
in alleys, in shadow, in doorways that keep quietly
asking to be opened so that nobody need stay
out of reach for long,
nor stand apart from each dawn's raising
of the daily stakes: setting against the certainty
of loss the possibility of wonder: winter, spring,
and summer nights to come not only for slow dying.

July Fourth

For Naomi

Rockets,
  for their splendor,
    release
in soaring
  arcs
    an instant's
expanded heat
  blown
    whistling over-
head, as if the world
  needed and would continue
    needing
such bom-
  bardment bursting in
    air, which doesn't hold
a candle
  as low,
    as lovely, as
preciously
  long
    as the snail-slow
uncurling
  tongue tip's brilliant
    orange-budded
stalk only your
  fierce attention
    stirs
out of the close
  hard ground, the glad-
    ioli newly-
ly
  at our
    feet.

Undeprived Yet of Memory,

while still my own contemporary,
I want to remember
that streak of orange-gold
I first saw flash
out of the carton you brought home – out
and into the bamboo cage
you had set beside it on the floor,
then shut the slotted door.
When that fleet fretting ball
of beak and feathers at last
slowed down like a held musical note
still mute
but visible on the staff-like perch, I saw
what I'd never seen
so close before: a thumb-sized
canary yellow scalp
parted in the middle
as in those speeded-up
scatter-brained Loony Tunes.
Could it possibly be, I wondered,
a toupee? What
huckster would bother with
a rug for the head of a bird? So
stubbornly unsinging and flawed
as it was, I suspected the seller
had stuck you with a lemon.
"Let's give it
a few days," you said,
then called out, "Wake up, Jacob!" –
three words that gave it gender, a name,
and a vocation it might not have had
had it flown out the window and tried
its luck among the bickering
mud-colored scavenger

sparrows in the yard you'd dubbed "rats
with wings" and which ever since have seemed so
much more furtive than free.
                              Then the few
unsung days grew into weeks,
until one morning we were awakened
by a startlingly sharp
whistle and trill
that held, then liquified
into a warble running breath-
takingly sweet. In summer,
now, it seems the only water
to be heard is in the bird's song.
In the company of others, when he sings,
they stop, lower their voices,
mouths open, struck dumb.

It Seems

the natural course of events can be depended on
to send things madly spinning
in the air, "topsy-turvy" we say, but
it's no longer child's play
when underfoot solid ground gives way and overhead
the peaceful mountain comes
to a rapid boil. Nature, out of retirement, bursts
far more than seams and collars and taxes
a fund of frailties we can't manage to keep
long afloat. One day what never was comes about;
what couldn't be, is. And there's no consolation
in foreseeing how the present will be
stood on its head before the final stitch frays.
No one's diminishment can serve
as a model to avoid, nor will
whoever consults a crystal ball eat
anything but glass. Even the old
nuisance you were quick to berate
in time will grow dear to you,
and what you can hardly abide
another moment you'll one day hear
yourself humbly mumbling
a patchwork prayer to be in the presence of once again,
as if precisely it — none other — had been
your choice all along,
not what was always wanted and denied, but
the handicap unwished for, given gratis, hobbling
heaven, withdrawn.

The United Way

photo — narrow, leonine, Hebraic, old
man's gentle, nearly feminine
smiling face, saying, "I don't know you
but I love you" — not anything you'd say,
                    yet something, the same
crease sea-weathered deep in the cheek, same

flint-
bright hint, part scrutiny, part
pity glistening the eye
when you would break into a smile, make me
look again and wonder: how, George,

this eerie likeness of you
found its way
twenty steel stories
above Embarcadero's smoked glass, flag-tier-
topped corporate towers, up
of all places, under the clock
on the sunlit lunchroom wall of
Cooley, Godward, Castro, Huddleson & Tatum,
Attorneys at Law. Here, a week into
reading proof and language — legalese —
leaves on the tongue a texture,
numb,
like wet cement. Now, through it, flash

Rezi, the years put in, now you receding
back in your reclining chair
those long August afternoons going
slowly rose, violet, wine-red
tincture in the sunsetting wave
suddenly evening, the airy

thinness we breathed
gaining volume, weight, we hardly
needing to speak...

As for talk of
poetry's luxury, necessity,
I see you amused, lean slant, mimic the rough
wry sound of those stern Maine lobstermen
standing knee-deep among their pots,
asking, "Much demand for it?"

How alive then
our laughter was indistinguishable from the light
of being here, necessity's
luxury, new as the taste of
water to one maddened with thirst,
hearing his leathery tongue strike
the roof of his mouth like a wooden clapper...
And we listen
when in a demotic more detailed
and deadly than ours, he speaks
words that, once said, set
in the bone. And laughter no water.

Each day earlier now, November's remote
sun's rays colder,
fog rolls in, covering blue
bay waters, sand beach, brilliant
bare light of summer days we used to head for,
downhill — rhythmic concord that's summoned
awake in walking, and the words that issue
in walking near water and that we pass through
more like windows than doorways
since we look in from so high
off our feet...

First light, then faces
brightening the light, sprawled park, sparkling
sea in which I sometimes sense
an almighty god, pitiless at particulars
and argument, asking, "Meaning?
You want meaning? My meaning
equals your gratitude!" and getting
away with it...

Eye moving forward, memory back
even to the anguished note fifty years in the voice,
a policeman leading you from a crowd to safety, pleading,
"Please, don't start trouble." How moved you were
by his concern for you, deeper, clearer
than words spoken only a moment ago, fallen in-
to the flood of the instant, making
itself felt only when toppling
                    forward in the froth...

Luckily, nearer, the ditch
calling for attention, rich earth winking blue
iris points as we walked the shore, circling
talk round and in
the same circle of the horizon, resonant
sound's kingdom, sound
of the words we need to spring
to our lips a new breathing in, a new singing out,
words that cannot live alone
any more than we can, hearing our own
voice through our throats, the voice of
others through our ears, saying
there is somewhere we want to go
where no sand blows over the spark of eyes
past the outer channel's curling lipped outrider, beyond
the far islands' depths now milling

your ashes, voice gone
where neither ear nor throat can hear
or hold
from scattering part of what we have
perhaps desperately come to
call immortal, meaning,
that is, unreturnable.

For George Oppen

Glimmers

Glimmers

of Leeuwenhoek's
drop

of water,
my first

lens,
tense, trans-

parent globe, condensed
sky

to see
through, continuable

point, free-
flowing window

you could draw
from the kitchen tap, through

an eye-
drop's worth, close-up, see

smooth white folded
nap, linen tablecloth's

woven waves, knotted
wood smoke, the moon

itself, pale window or marble
well, another

matter. And what
worlds more

wondrous with each downward drop-
let blooming

a knot
open in the grain

of vision! And from that wood
a leaf's threaded net-

work of lacy veins
retracing those in the hand

holding it, and the eye
stunned wide

at twelve seeing
Tchelitchew's celestial tree,

drawing radiant embryo
boys out of fiery air, take

root, live melting or molding luminous
foliage, their nerve-waving faces'

peeled eyeballs a shimmer
of molten ganglia, soaked bloody

space aglow, the inner
core heat consuming stars...

What were they beginnings of
but faces of dread

and desire still
to come — summer's ice-

blossom cornea, crystallized,
staring

within
the webbed wood's center

at her whose reach they elude
yet are drawn to, surround,

silently mouthing,
warning, wooing, as if

calling for help,
and plunging

were about to be-
come soaring,

and midway is
tangled branches, brain, stem.

How brightly
expectant

they hover!
as if in a gathering

sense that being seen
by such unblinking

eyes of air and water
is to shine, be given

power. And he
who in that light

sees you — see now
through his eyes

the many-eyed sun-
flower

head of a fly
through a microscope,

its flickering
green-gold

iridescent wing
cells like tiny

conical bricks
in a wall that flew! Imagine —

protein-bonded vapor
spun

over eons
into tissue

withstanding
swipes of wind, hand, spun

out of microbes like those
thriving

in a waterdrop — live
hair, hook-tailed, locked looping

as curved sweeping scimitars of
Arabic calligraphy

your father wrote out for you
one day in rapid flowing

script. Were they, too,
linked or fleeting

strands of barely familiar
code all the more

dream-like for being
so close at hand? Might those

lenses once have been
steadily concentrated on

by the hand and consciousness
of free-thinking, stubborn,

damned Spinoza
dividing infinity

into axioms
and rays

of rational harmony? Divinity
embodied in a mathematics

deemed heretical, but,
to a boy, so chaste, incorporeal,

I couldn't begin to understand,
nor why heresy? Only that

this gentle excommunicant
and terror of Talmudic rabbis

I studied under
and hid

my reading from,
called by his fellow townsfolk

when not trying to lynch him,
"This Jew,

the only man among us
who talks like Christ,"

too solitary and shy
for a hero,

this feverish, tubercular
silkworm in his cocoon,

could for hours be totally
absorbed watching spiders

battle in corners of his attic room
in Amsterdam. Eternity looked on

that world, too,
abandoned by the sun

from where Vermeer's poured milky
glistening

pearl-
drop earring's

an eye
still

shining through
sand and pigment, beckoning

testament to the untouchable
blue

veil,
light and air. Blessed

Baruch, in the rays
of that illumination permitting

what is forbidden, did he
grind for twenty years, for failing

Dutch patrons' eyes, lenses to fine
dust before breathing himself

an early grave
on February 25, 1677, anniversary,

two hundred seventy years later, of my birth.
Axiom: in the beginning

Elohim
created by contracting

Light Without End
to nothing — *tzimtzum* — but a dimensionless

dot, the heavens and earth,
in a mastery so absolute as to be

invisible. Proof: visible and
invisible, the hazardous dread-

fulness of reaching twelve convincing me
I'd reach no more

than twenty-five, and am already dogging
twice that, dogged by

a weight as of a sea
that brought us

here, tide pushed on by
tides behind, pulled

forth by tides forward...ocean
given different names

on the different shores
it washes, serving

the pin-
hole

hollow pupil
of the chambered nautilus

as eyeball. There, down under
then, regain

our sight? and, between
dropping

or diving, as we choose,
go

into better
armed than empty-

handed? So the body, fed
on illness — if the inner disturbance is

great enough — creates
its health, increasingly

fragile, increasingly
complex, a higher order. Imagine —

two particles, once in contact,
separated even to the ends of

the universe, change
instantaneously when

a change in one of them
occurs. So,

heart in mouth, feel
the speeding music's

measure slow, if not for which,
how would you know the lovely

touch of time's caressing,
shapely, shiftless

body? How
slipped

through your fingers it may
be placed in your hands again...

"Water," said David at six,
"burns fire." With that. Now

between dimming and flaring
glimmers backing up, see

the cardboard-stiff black cat
found at curbside

you buried deep at night
in the raving widow's grape arbor –

our fort and arsenal
against the huge

blunt cars, like waves of
invaders in those World War II years –

their Atlas-
bearing hoods aimed speedily

down streets so wide,
what hordes did they imagine,

on what air-
swollen wheels, would have the right of way? –

breaking up our games: the wild
delirious animal

elasticity running
a batted ball

down barely
within reach. Not till

now seeing those hidden
dangers: late

one summer afternoon
in those days that seemed to stay

aloft forever, beneath
the lightning-

winged Mobil Pegasus
hoof-raised

three floors up, outside
our bedroom window,

its silver-blue fluorescent
tubes not yet lit

for neon night-
flight, high

on running bases, Joey, showing off, holds
the oily orange gasoline pump's

hose close
up for a look, spills

a drop, screams,
clutching the runny

sunset flame in his eye, jumping
to put it out.

53

Or those chimes
of the eagerly awaited

immaculate Good Humor
truck, fragrant of vanilla,

on that, or another, sunny day,
which struck

Eddie's lovely blond five-year-old sister
down, hers the only eyes

closed, head hard-wrenched
far away in the light of the sun clean-

clawing the carnivorous street.
Weeks later, dug up

the cat, saw the frightful
white worms wriggling

inside the shape that had been, gut-
emptying gleams

dimly even now
lighting that darkness continuously

tunneling from birth. And I remember,
I remember as if having to go under

for air, not the wind waking
but the low roar

of years — night, solitude
no blindfold

but an eye conscious
of being an eye,

inheriting the past
of your nights and the awful

mounting dread at the courage needed
to be born.

Through an opening
bloody or bright,

you enter yourself
as you enter the night: birth

either to choose or wither
on the vine...

Years later, feel the eerie
undersea tug again,

reading in Ferenczi's *Thalassa*,
when the primal oceans receded, drying,

and our gill-breathing ancestors evolved
organs for breathing

air and protecting the embryo —
the danger not of drowning

but desiccation —
and with seeking the aquatic

existence of which they had
been deprived, came the impulse

for the first time
to penetrate

into the body
of another. Sexual

combat begun as a struggle
for moisture? Fucking

to be intra-
uterine again? For the parasite's

fear of birth and the pleasure,
finally, of surmounting that danger?

If, in the child, sucking, touching,
being touched, looking, being looked at, provide

complete satisfaction, in the adult
looking, kissing, sucking serve

genital eruption.
Unless the pulse of

gladness gather, quicken
periodically to be

released in rhythmic rapture,
the eye would be absorbed

in endless looking, the mouth in sucking,
the hand in touching, leaving the body

open
to attack.

Does limiting intensest pleasure
to a single organ increase

efficiency and make adapting to threat —
to catastrophe even — possible?

Might there be, then, no part of the body
not represented in the genital,

when in the moment of libido
back-flow occurs that ineffable

feeling, "oceanic bliss," bringing
solace to the struggle,

giving strength and inducement to
further toil?…meaning, for instance,

now. For isn't this
the future you dreamed of all

the time? — small, frail
vessel now

thrown
together at sea even as the journey —

and not over
gentle

blue water always nor through
long lingering low-

lidded looks
beckoning just a little

ahead of your reach — even as the journey
proceeds, eye meat

eating the meat of vision, demi-
paradise but for our blindness,

not its absence, turned back
each moment into history bringing us

shakily from
sleep and roughly to

our feet before sending us
flying – the eye not

quick, not
physical enough to see

no break in the dream
dreamed by a single being wherein

all the dream creatures also dream
of no longer dreaming

but of living *in* the dream.
In the heaven of Indra

is a network of pearls
so arranged, if one is looked at,

all the others are seen
reflected in it, each

made of all the others,
each link's

pull on the whole
moiling

seafloor-yoked
ensemble any midnight could steal

seafloor-yoked
ensemble any midnight could steal

the heart out of
any or all

our hands held together, desiring
what never was, anxious

for what is no longer...
Between stars and salt of the deep

dispersed body whose
skin we are —

though the way repeatedly
forgotten and heart's blood hinting

home, sung to
in crooned or stuttered

music that never had reason
to begin

any more
than to end — all

oceans to it are
one

drop.
To trace beyond

would be trying to tell
the story of the sea, dark

blue depths, darker within and farther in,
nothing.

I don't want to hear any more
about eternity...

This moment
is not enough? — then

eternity won't be either.

After Rumi

NOTE

These poems are "after" Rumi in several senses of the word: in time, on the trail of, as a continuing afterlife of the originals. Grateful as I am to the earlier translations by Nicholson and Arberry, I feel their Victorian style hampers what seems to me to be crucial to Rumi: his quickness and agile brevity in making connections between dialectical ideas and opposed imagery. In physical terms, this is what the whirling dance of the Mevlevi dervishes denotes: the living vortex of opposites, wobbling yet conjoined.

Though Rumi was already a master teacher at the age of thirty-seven in the theological academy founded by his father, he became an ardent disciple of Shams-al-Haqqi-Tabrizi, the vagabond dervish who taught Rumi about the Wine of Love and the whirling dance that offered the union beyond opposites. Without setting aside his own Islamic faith, Rumi could say, "The religion of Love is like no other."

In order to let us and himself drink and become intoxicated with the awareness of the Beloved One's presence, Rumi will humor, cajole, berate, confound, and shock us. This quality seems to be set off by the keenest sense of paradox, which explodes our safeguarded reasonableness in the face of an ever-shifting reality. Often in a kind of high comic frenzy (to my mind, not unlike that induced by someone like Lenny Bruce, had he been a Sufi), Rumi traps us in our assumptions, outwits our escape, and drops us, accompanied by the sound of our own laughter, into not a void but a vortex of the here and now, the recreative energy in the immediate instant.

With this in mind, I have tried to make Rumi's lines swifter, leaner, more flexible, to better express his sense of simultaneous contraries, or his non-sense, and have felt free to use a more colloquial idiom. I think of these not so much as adaptations as transfusions of a continuing source, in keeping with the impromptu ecstatic state that infused their original utterance.

"Every Form You See..."

Every form you see has its origin in the placeless world;
Even if the form should disappear, its origin lasts forever.
Every shape you've seen, every phrase you've heard —
Don't despair that they've disappeared; it only seems so.
Since the spring is constant, its branch continually gives water;
Since neither runs out, why this sorrow?
Imagine the soul as a fountain, and these visible things as rivers:
While the fountain flows, the rivers run.
Put sorrow out of your head and keep drinking this river.
Don't think of the water as finite; this water is endless.
From the moment you entered the world, a ladder
Was set before you so that you might escape.
First you were mineral, later plant,
Then animal; how could this be such a secret?
Look at the body, a heap from the dust pit —
　　　how perfect it has grown!
When you've moved on from being human,
　　　you'll no doubt become an angel;
After that, you're finished with this world.
Move on then from being an angel; enter that ocean
Where one drop turns countless oceans.

"Dawn Has Arrived…"

Dawn has arrived and drawn its gleaming blade, and morning
    comes with the whiteness of camphor.
The Sufi of the skies has torn his blue robe to the navel.
After being routed, the Rumi of day regains his power and
    has dragged the Zangi of night from the throne.
From the direction that the joyful Turk and the sorrowful Hindu
    arrived, there is a constant going and coming, but the way
    has never been charted.
To where has the army of the Abyssinian king retreated?
From where so suddenly have helmeted troops arrived?
Who can catch a whiff of this invisible road?
Night is surprised at how its face is blackened; day is
    surprised at being so bright.
Earth is surprised to find half of it is grass and the
    other half always grazing,
Half become eater and half the eaten, half thirsting to be
    pure and the other half hungry for garbage.
Cupbearer, today we're all your guests; pour the wine
    that purifies; only new joy can throw off anxiety.

"Just the Other Day…"

Just the other day the fire whispered to the smoke, "The wood
  can't relax without me; with me it is happy.
It knows my worth and thanks me, because the wood now knows
  there is something to be gained through burning.
Having been bound and knotted from top to bottom, the wood
  is freed into nonbeing, the knots untied.
Welcome, my flame-eating friend, my passer-away, my most
  faithful witness."
See how heaven and earth are pawns of existence; escape from
  the blindness of the one and the blueness of the other.
So long as sperm remained sperm and wasn't released in seminal rushes,
  there could be neither the forest's height nor the face's beauty.
Bread and soup digested in the stomach are turned into imagination
  and reason.
So long as black rock was not upheaved in the mother lode, it
  couldn't become gold and silver.
Eyes open but still unconscious, you have fallen asleep as the water
  of Khidar splashes beside you.
Wake up, wake up, and grab the cup that is nearer than the jugular vein!

"A Hundred Drums Beating..."

A hundred drums beating inside our hearts — their sound
    we will hear tomorrow.
Cotton wool in the ear, hair in the eye — they're tomorrow's worry,
    the constancy of sorrow.
Throw love's flame into this cotton wool, like Hallaj and
    the other consumed ones;
Or else why keep flame and cotton wool together? Opposites
    don't survive.
Since the meeting is near, welcome its presence.
For us, dying is the fullness of arrival; if, for you, that's
    reason for mourning, leave now;
As much as this world is a prison, the collapse of prisons
    is something to celebrate;
And the High One whose prison is so delightful — how much
    more so will be His private courtyard!
Don't look for permanence in this prison, since permanence
    itself hasn't ever believed in it.

"If You Break Our Harps..."

If you break our harps, O High One, there are thousands
    of other harps here.
Since we've fallen into such hands, what matter
    if we lose our harp and flute?
Friend, if all the world's drums and harps were destroyed,
    there are many more hidden ones;
Their beating and strumming mounts to the skies, even
    if not into the ears of the deaf.
All the world's lamps and candles flickering out
    would be no cause for sorrow; wick and flint are still here.
Songs are spindrift on the face of the sea; no pearl
    appears on the surface.
But the graceful curl of spindrift mirrors the pearl, reflection
    of the reflection of the gleam that is upon us.
Songs are branches of the urge toward union, though
    branch and root are not the same.
Close your mouth and open the inner window in order to be
    closer to that union.

"You Said, 'Don't Bother Me Anymore!'…"

You said, "Don't bother me anymore!" That phrase of yours —
    "Don't bother me!" — is my desire.
And your dismissing me: "Leave, the King is not at home!"
    That brusque command and rudeness of the doorman
    are my desire.
To the hand of every living beggar there clings
    a few precious filings; that
    quarry and that mine are my desire.
Like Jacob mourning the lost face of Joseph,
    somewhere in Egypt is my desire.
Without you, the city is a prison I prowl in;
    mountain and desert are my desire.
Sick of ingratitude and complaint, the raving
    and whirling of drunkards is my desire. More
Eloquent than the nightingale, my tongue is weighted down
    with envy, and despondency is my desire.
Last night, lamp in hand, the sheik roamed the city, crying,
    "I'm sick of ogres and demons — a man is my desire."
Voices answered, "We've all searched — he can't be found."
He replied, "He who can't be found is my desire."

"FOR AS LONG AS THE BELOVED'S FACE..."

For as long as the Beloved's face is with us, living is
    a continual celebration.
Where friends rejoice together, there in the middle of the house
    is a wide open plain.
And where desire is realized, there one thorn
    is worth the whole harvest.
When we sleep with our heads on the road leading to the Beloved,
    our pillows and blankets are the Pleiades.
On the Night of Power, when we're woven into the curls of
    the Beloved's hair, power runs through us.
When the reflection of that beauty shines forth, mountains
    and valleys are silk and brocade.
When we search in the breeze for a trace of it, the breeze
    echoes with harp and flute.
When we write the Name in the dust, every mote is a dancing
    dervish.
When we chant it over the fire, the flame turns cool as water.
Why make a short story long? When we speak the Name into the
    void, something comes out of nothing.

"O Lovers, Lovers, Today..."

O lovers, lovers, today we've fallen into a whirl-
    pool: who knows how to swim?
Though the torrent's flow should overrun its banks and every
    wave raise a hump like a camel, why should the waterfowl
    worry? It's the airborne bird that should be wary.
Faces lit with awe, we're schooled in crest
    and seafloor and know that swelling
    rivers and flood mean more
    teeming fishes.
Old one, hand us a towel; water, make way.
In every head this wind stirs a different passion; drunkenly, madly,
    you draw me on — won't you say where to?
Wherever you go, I'm with you still, you who are my eyes
    and their brightness; if you wish, draw me down
    to drunkenness; if you will,
    light me to annihilation.
Look: the world is like Mount Sinai, and we, like Moses,
    are tongue-tied wanderers; every moment, a revelation arrives
    and breaks the mountain to pieces.
One part becomes dark green, one part lily-white; one grain
    becomes a pearl, another ruby and amber.
You who want to see Him, look at this mountain chain
    of His. O mountain, what wind has blown down you?
    We've grown giddy with the echo.
O gardener, gardener, why have you come to uproot us?
If we've pilfered your grapes, you've left us penniless!

"You Who Are Not Kept Anxiously Awake..."

You who are not kept anxiously awake for love's sake, sleep on.
In restless search for that river, we hurry along; you
  whose heart such anxiety has not disturbed, sleep on.
Love's place is out beyond the many separate sects; since
  you love choosing and excluding, sleep on.
Love's dawn cup is our sunrise, his dusk our supper; you
  whose longing is for sweets and whose passion is for
                                        supper, sleep on.
In search of the philosopher's stone, we are melting
  like copper; you whose philosopher's stone is cushion
                                    and pillow, sleep on.
I have abandoned hope for my brain and head; you who wish for
  a clear head and fresh brain, sleep on.
I have torn speech like a tattered robe and let words go; you
  who are still dressed in your clothes, sleep on.

"Look Out, Don't Slip..."

Look out, don't slip, the roads behind and ahead are slick
                                                with blood.
 These days there are more body snatchers than money
                                                snatchers.
They mean to rob people senseless, so what will they do
 with those who can't make sense of themselves?
Don't think you're unnoticed and without takers;
 the marketplace is after gold, and the ore is you.
The Prophet said, "Men are mines." Though you find treasure,
 you don't find a life to go with it.
Look out, don't sleep, a nimble, feathery thief is on the way.

"Look at the Silly Prince..."

Look at the silly prince, with his little horse and little saddle,
    sly and self-serving, his head wrapped in golden cloth.
Since he's not convinced of ending, he boasts, "Where is it?"
    And from all directions the end rushes to him, calling,
"Here I am! Jackass, what is all that galloping about? those
    mustaches, that sneering nose, that self-satisfied bluster?
Where is happiness? To whom did you give your blanket? Now
    a brick is your pillow, your mattress the ground.
Say goodbye to eating and sleeping. Say hello to breaking and
                                   scattering."
    Body, that's you; that prince, me.
Shams-al-Haqqi Tabrizi, you are yourself that living water,
    and what can see and feel that stream but the fluid eye?

"What Kind of King Creates..."

What kind of King creates a king out of dust, for the sake of
      one or two beggars makes Himself into a beggar?
Who pleads like the poor and wretched, "Give me a loan,"
      so that He may give you a kingdom and design a throne?
Those He passes by die — and those who aren't yet come to life.
He creates a pain and a cure for the pain.
When He condenses the wind, it becomes water;
When He vaporizes water, it's air.
Don't despise the world; because of that, the world is dying.
Men rave about the alchemy that turns copper into gold; why
      not rave about the mind that turns copper into alchemy?
If there are locks and bolts on your cravings, don't give up;
      keep looking for the sweetshop the Sweetheart keeps open.
Without pen or outline here in the place of appearances, the One
      who makes so many lovely forms for us makes
      many lovers and beloveds of us — such forms
      the Formless creates for itself!

If your heart is iron, don't regret its hardness;
      it's being polished into the clearest of mirrors.
When you leave your friends and go under the dust,
      He'll make the snakes and ants far lovelier companions.
Look into the pit of the body — what ravishing sights
      He instantly creates there!
If you want to know where you come from, cut
      open your chest and tell what you see there.
Eat the grapes, but don't interrogate the garden.
He makes thousands of fountains from one stone; inside of
      a stone have you found any water?
What we see He makes from the unseen; out of the
      limitless came these limits; out of No,
      numberless Yeses.

Look at two rivers of light flowing from two pieces of fat;
    don't be astonished He turns a rod into a snake.
Examine these two ears: can you find where a hole becomes
                                                    hearing?
    Rave about Him who allows a hole to hear.
He gives the body's house a spirit and makes it master;
    when He kills the master, He makes him another house.
Though the master's house goes under the dust, his heart is
    carried to higher places.
To those who believe only their eyes, the master is gone,
    but He is making the master a suit of a different cut.
Be quiet now, quit praising and praying, so that
    He may make of you prayer and praise.

"When You Carry My Casket…"

When you carry my casket on the day of my death,
Don't think I'm sorry to leave this world;
Don't mourn for me and cry, "No more, no more…"
You'd be sadly mistaken.
When you see my casket, don't cry, "Gone, gone…"
Union and reunion are mine in that hour.
When you lower me into the grave, don't say, "Goodbye,
    goodbye…"
The grave is a curtain obscuring the nearness of paradise.
After seeing the going down, imagine the coming up.
Has setting ever put an end to sunrise?
To you it seems like a sinking, but is really a rising.
What seed planted didn't finally grow?
Then why this doubt of yours about a seed of the human?
What bucket ever sent down didn't come up brimful?
Why should Joseph of the spirit complain about the well?
When you shut your mouth on this side, open it on the other.

From
The Darkest Continent
(1967)

The Gold Coast

And so it is Africa we each seek after all.
After watching toothless lions shrug through fire
and, flawlessly as snow, tinsel-coifed firs
ward winter mildly off lavender walls,
we trade some wax roses and a shawl
                                    and then retire.

It is the mandrill's flagrant roar along the glades
and deserts galloping astride the grinning blades
of slave and sultan prostrate on the sand
where parentheses of muezzin arms raise
"Allah is highest."
                    The blackamoor magdalenes
of Marrakesh mince up, laughing, to their beds,
and love, the darkest continent, ascends to morning.

Tetanus gouts the marketplace; mulattoes and bees
sting the smoking oxen's eyes where a sunstruck beggar reeks
lice and palm wine, the cataracts of his eyes,
lepers to the light, his turban coiling
the sun, cobra-hooded around his head.

Off Ghana, where stripped crews race their bumboat cotton,
Gold Coast Spartans appease the gods of fire and stone,
drum and trident, Assyrian script foam…
O blood-bound sails of Saladin unfurling.

THE WAY BACK

Those white-hot ports drifting
through flour, baking like bread
in the sun; that ship —
I have been thinking about its hull,
sun-slick between Azores and Lagos,
the hold drumming
with the absolute, impossible cargo
that would not see the light,
the crude lyre I was given —
a rum crate, four saw blades over slots
my fingers cut themselves on,
they plucked so hard...
that too left behind.

These days, living near the smell
but not the sight,
I walk up Whitehall Street
toward the river, where it ended,
keeping an eye
for a slim white prow above the harbor sheds.
Part of me, having said it
once — and badly —
knows we have nothing more
to say to each other.
Knows this, turning.

PARK WEST

1

Sultry as bedposts, the subway lamps
shine. Beside him, padding up the stairs
like a seeing-eye dog, a draft romps
ahead, lifts their dresses in pairs
from behind, then dashes back to be petted...
his thoughts, hands almost, palms wet.
For all the good they do,
he might as well be blind.
Out of the corner of his eye
he watches life going in all directions,
like his mind.

2

Central Park steams
like a jungle, each streetlamp
a dust bowl. No leaf, he leans,
feeling his sapped roots rooted to thin air.
Nothing that cares grows here
but bellies, bribes, habits,
and hefty gutter rats that gorge on pyramids of filth
left out overnight by the Negro janitor.
On the walk: nylon flash,
mother-of-pearl, scintillant swansdown
puckers just inside the knee...
that's where his mind hinges.
Can he make the fringes kick higher, faster,
like that night in Dakar or Mozambique
when, for once, his mania came close
to getting a bellyful...
then blacked out?

3

Wondering how much to give in or pull
back, astigmatic as a bull,
his lust squints, spies through white cashmere
the thick, ogling horn-rims of a black brassiere.
Burly, lounging in a doorway like a cop, night
pokes this ash-heap Harlem with a flashlight,
where each deaf-mute, pop-eyed soul drags
for a fix, jabs
once, sees the stars pop one by one
and time fan out light-years on the head of a pin.

4

Soul tapering
to fingertips, he wants to be that hidalgo
wrapped in flaming emerald who walks on air in Toledo...
but only death will make it so.
Trying to think of the past, his mind stretches
up the Congo — shore lights swirling
on the current, on the deck,
blades churning a feather bed of foam
and, in him, fear
by rote: "Don't look back. Do it here. Here!"
And that was nowhere.

5

Relieved, a light goes on
in his mind, then off, then on again,
like a firefly he used to cup in his hand
as a child, make a wish, let go.
The way a Negro's hand turning palm up shades
slowly from coal-black, bronze, to light,
dawn's fist unclenches.

CROSSWINDS

1

In Kivu province Hutu vassals turn
on their Watusi lords. "A thousand souls a day
clot the riverbanks," say the newspapers.
Here in America I watch the sooty water towers
over Harlem sweat with a mind to burst.
The landlord, in his bar
just long enough to count last night's receipts,
will head home to the sterilized suburbs.
In Central Park, smutty defoliated trees
fidget with omens ruffling the uniforms
of nurse and nun, the very pointed branches ready
to spring, white America pierced through the heart
by a rank forest stalking its inheritance
on all fours, watered by falls
natives called "The Smoke That Thunders."

2

Favorites of the god of Rwanda,
whose ancestors rose from dry Ethiopian plains,
driving before them their longhorns, sacred Nganda,
crossed the Nile and Nubian desert to find
their promised land and fall on masters
of pygmy hunters, Hutu, stunted diggers,
tillers of primal mud, reapers of cassava and manioc,
who built Watusi's rattan huts and planted maize
on the terraced hillsides, served the milk of divinity
to the slim dandy leaning in his sedan chair
dreaming of a lion's haunch, a winged torso,
each slender, sable limb longing to become a sphinx.

3

America, hugging her knees in the corner,
glued to the baby talk of TV,
once the only daughter of heaven,
now won't hear the fish-breathing Mongol
panting outside the window, wanting in.
White-bread-body, waitress-face, the virgin
still wants her way or will not come out.
Something she has let go undone,
lest the deed rob her innocence, turns
in her now, turns the gripped image of purity
into the murder of her neglect...
The ego, breaking up, clings to its own hair;
the only green within memory, it seems,
an avocado at her window leans,
dreaming of sunflowers in Spain.

4

Unhusked like chaff to Hutu flails,
Hamite stalks blow back on the wind into nothingness.
Tall and tall lengthens the shadow of their fall,
hunters turned prey in a further turning of the game.
High jumpers of the veldt,
beehive-coifed — in profile, Pharaohs —
who by courtly wit and honeyed verses
decreed laughter unfit for such nobles as they...
a crudeness of slaves.

5

"Harlequins they are by nature, high-spirited
and given to bouts of wild abandon,
dancing and chanting savage rhythms
unlike their Christian neighbors
who are in bed by midnight."

6

In Lagos, the arms of rancid women in tin shacks,
dung and drunkenness, the moon's white stain
and starlight twinkling on the teeth of a native,
mouth open, gurgling in a ditch —
the voyage has come to that.
Then morning, a mammy sashays to market,
the fluted jug on her head, round and full
as her body brimming over, the living sun.
Night, the engines drumming
a highlife below deck, move the shining stevedores
to flex and free what awaited them
in the thicket of the dance, giving in
as though an easy ecstasy always within reach
might open a circle and nature, drunkenly big-hearted,
make herself felt like a giantess
at whose laughter everything dances.

Shells, red ankle bells
heel clean the dusty air;
a spear of ebony each limb,
golden headdress, lion's mane
sweeps hills and grassland
for the stride of antelope,
the spring of the cat.

7

"Like children they are,
delighting in the whims and flights of imagination
over the regularity of commerce.
At the bottom of their hearts
what they really fear is pedantry.
In the hands of pedants they die of grief."

Proud hunter necks bowed into yokes
to haul bales of booty to his ships,
seditious Indians of Hispaniola
moved Columbus to write his queen,
"Madame, the innocents have risen. Send hounds
and milder Negroes who delight in such labor."

And the captain, fearing the blind slave
would infect his fellows, cast him overboard.
Others went blind, others overboard.
The affliction grew below deck
till every living soul aboard,
crew and slave, white and black,
each went dark inside.

8

Watusi, blood brother to Somali, Galla, Fulani,
Masai, Mandingo, herded into kraals
that penned their royal cattle — pure pedigree,
horns sand-polished, coats rubbed with the butterfat
their udders gushed, each cow attended by a youth
robed in bark cloth, who never spoke to it but softly,
catching its dung on a woven straw mat.

9

Set sail from London a hundred Englishmen
for Virginia, earth's only paradise,
to seeke not talke, nor faith, nor common worke,
but dig and wash, refine and load
the bright bullion, gold...
Found fair meadows and goodly tall trees,
with such fresh waters running through the woods
they were almost ravished with the sight thereof,
prairies so broad and level
if a man lay on his back, he lost sight of the earth.

10

And though their kingdom lay open to slavers
hauling natives from the markets of Zanzibar,
the Mwami's loyal spearmen held to ranks
and swung the Arab horsemen to the Persian Gulf.
They must have heard their serfs grumble
and point to the iron collars biting into the blacks,
whose bodies so packed the ships bound for the new Americas
the visionary Jefferson said, "I tremble for my country
when I reflect that God is just."

11

Who cared to know the rhythms of a dance unfulfilled,
coiling in the chest to kill or be killed?
Gentle Livingstone opened Africa
to sanitary reformers, inventors of telegraphs and steam engines,
Christ and commerce, the soldiers of Sevastopol.
Soon the saber-rattling Kaiser, the League and Leopold,
locusts lit on a leaf, woke the sleeping giant;
and Africa's rhino head crashed the twentieth century.

12

Pink, polyethylene flamingoes add an air
of make-believe to the lawns of Dixie;
they step on one light foot
and disturb no one's sleep.
On street corners in New York,
Negroes in tight suits
flick copies of *Muhammad Speaks*
at strolling couples, like switchblades.
A glowering fury spreads to quiet country lanes
where coal-black wrought-iron stableboys
rush out to meet you, noose in hand.

Three Portraits

SELF-PORTRAIT, CÉZANNE

My dear son, Paul,
how grateful I am, for you
are the true genius in the family.
You rescue my affairs from confusion.
Here, where the climate is most favorable
to the expansion of metals, wine merchants'
purses, and beer-drinkers' bellies,
on the river's edge, the motifs are
plentiful, as are the pretensions
of fools…not unlike Paris,
where those back-stabbers and scribbling
Dreyfusards such as the traitorous
Zola fester and lower
their voices, though I can still hear them call
your good Mama *The Ball* — as if
she kept me on a chain and I was not
a dull stonemason of slippery glimpses.
The exceptions among them — there must be some —
don't make themselves known.

For myself, when fatigue backs me to the wall,
my only course is to turn and face the wall and stare
down its blankness. Stick to it —
stick to it at all costs! though
I sometimes think I would paint differently
if the Louvre put a wall at my disposal.
Then the weight I feel before the masters
would lift and with it that which my poor self is
bound to, leaving me in moments of greatest tension
to let my fingers sense the straining
threads running through them and look
to it as best they can. What's left
are a few patches on bare canvas.
Gauguin? Van Gogh? Poachers and lunatics

make things easy for themselves!
The Louvre is the book we must learn to read.

Yesterday the crafty Abbé Roux,
wanting to get his clerical hooks into me,
took a carriage and came to hunt me up.
He's a cretin. I promised to see him
at the Catholic College. I won't go.
I must learn to use the remaining time like a tree.
Ten strokes of the brush in one day is quite a lot
until the space between colored intervals gradually
dissolves. Others may be content with the sheen of flesh-
toned fruit or the light that flits
coquette-like along wet surfaces.
My strokes are intent
on more elusive
blocks, bone, the inner
grid and gristle on which things stand.
Coherence is what matters. If I find it
in tatters, I will gather in tatters and build with
tiny staggered layers of sun-
lit air, the abyss I breathe, my inheritance.

So from what chaos holds I must take,
set down, yoke together, fix
all that's scattered, flickering
tones, shades, locking hands. There must be
not a single link too loose, a hole
through which the emotion, light, or truth
may escape. I must use many different blues
to link the near and far. It is like
being born with blue
eyes, like Renoir.
Unlike him, I am not enamored of the "beautiful"
harmonies of those who have gone
before, though theirs may be a way
for some to follow.

For all that, I cannot
arrive at or realize in art
the intensity of my senses.
I know only time and meditation
tend to modify vision little
by little. In the end comes
understanding, though it's sad
our means of expression follows
on feebleness and decay.
Hopeless sadness in that
all we see and rejoice in
dies for us as soon
as it's seen. Sad hope
that what we now look at will be
there forever.

Perhaps it is not to satisfy
that desire but to create new ones
through shimmering
spacious hallways, cobalt rocks,
blue sky, sea and mountain,
pathway to a shadowy corner of the garden
where after steady labor solidly
on the earth the old gardener rests.
With his silver-
white beard, yellow-orange hat,
he is Titian
stepped out of his frame,
like all my beloved ones,
Rubens, Rembrandt, Veronese, Delacroix.
In the now-empty spaces they leave
their echo. This does not diminish me,
from whom a live tradition might yet spring,
I, your father, Paul Cézanne,
who am nothing.

Paul Celan, Before Accepting the Bremen Prize

Breath by breath, so
breathing has used you,
so have the vanished
found a way through
a parted Red Sea,
come nearer...

Word by word now
is writing a making
naught of yes and no,
a whitening of hues,
a making with no
beginning, no end,

a wandering, empty
desert-mute
middle
facing both ways
at once, Egypt, Sinai,
having your death while still alive

and never the same
death twice in light-

blinding Paris...

From here, then, go
back there where
those who would have done away
with you and your history
now offer you a place
in theirs?
           Blood spilled by

a generation of butchers
is not sawdusted under
by an evening's good intentions...

Remember one night in Hamburg, walking
along the Reeperbahn, when suddenly a great cry
arose in the street. A woman in a Volkswagen had run over
a dog that had broken away from its owner. Cries of "O
my God! I didn't mean to do that!" and "O my God, what
have I done!"

   How they carried on...
  who can neither live
 without you
    to burn or to baptize...
        So eternally
are they the one thing in your heart you have
to hate, they have won —
they, their fatherland, your forefathers'
Father making you leaven
in the ovens, commanding you to be
more merciful than he, and nowhere near
enough to see or believe
except as toying, teasing, mad-
dog devouring...

So stammer the bitter,
hammer the master
speech left to you
down as you go, dis-
member it, worm
from within, cripple
the killer's tongue, cross-
hatch each syllable touched
with scar tissue. Raise
corpses from the welts, let

97

the risen corpses fire
their double loads
of terror and torture
before they were
made ash and air.
                        Might it be better
if your mouth was set
                        higher
                                    than your eyes
and your voice ran
                        ahead, upward
                                    groping for
finer, less visible thread, cries of the
risen
        to be lowered
                        here within reach, smoke
souls calling
                down
                        their ridicule? —
                Evil evil evil the living bark and leaves
                and budding tree of the flowering
                God in whose future all are
                stacked cords of wood.

Go, walk through the mountains
standing on your head...
Underneath you'll have
                        heaven
in which to fall.

Go home,
                burning
down, love the candle
your mother's hand did not
live to light.

Go,
thank the Germans
in Germany, in German,
while thinking of
the cloud folk in the air
they breathe all around,
the smoke still in it.
Remind them,
they need reminding:

> "Ladies and gentlemen,
> *denken und danken,*
> thinking and thanking,
> have the same origin.
> Whoever follows
> their sense will come to
> 'remember, remembrance,
> be mindful, devotion.'
>
> From this perspective,
> allow me to
> thank you."

Re: Emily

Afraid to own a body,
am alive, I guess,
ashamed, I hide, ask
no other thing but
what the wind blows
bringing an unaccustomed
wine I cannot buy, it is not
sold but with a grief I
cannot live with, or meet
the spring unmoved, cannot
want it more or feel it
cautious, scanning
my little life, sufficing,
not reaching thee, dreading
that first robin so that dwells
in possibility whereon he rides
cleaving my mind, a funeral
in my brain I feel with both my hands
to find the words to every thought
I gain, I give myself to, I get so
I grope for before I know I
have been hungry all the years I have
no cause to be awake but time
to hate the things that I call mine,
when nothing more will do,
but a king who does not speak,
who laps the miles, lives on,
while I measure every grief
I meet and never hear
the word *escape*, never lose
less than twice and notice
people disappear while I play
at riches to appease and reckon
when I count at all,

I rob the woods and winds
within and see the better
in the dark, clearer, the grave
and sunset in decrepit
flower, singing daily.
I shall know why
when time is over
and not murmur at the last
that should not be so sad
but sing to use the waiting and think
just how my shape will rise and stand
in the longest hour...
                    I've stopped
being theirs and take
my power in my hand. "I want, I want"
pleads with all its life,
"if this be fading."

Composition in Fournier by Walker & Swenson, Book Typographers. Designed by Allan Kornblum. This book was printed on acid-free paper at Inter-Collegiate Press and was sewn in signatures to ensure durability.